The Little Book on Culture: Building and Sustaining a Positive Workplace

By Mark Lowe

Acknowledgement:

I would like to express my deepest gratitude to my wife Annie for her unwavering support and encouragement throughout the process of writing this book. Her love and understanding have been a constant source of inspiration for me.

I would also like to extend my thanks to all the businesses that I have worked with over the years, as they have provided me with valuable insights and experiences that have helped shape my understanding of organizational culture.

Lastly, I would like to thank my readers for their interest in this book. It is my hope that the ideas and strategies presented within these pages will help organizations of all sizes and types build and sustain positive cultures that benefit everyone involved.

Introduction:

- Explanation of what organizational culture is
- The impact of culture on employee motivation, productivity, and retention
- The significance of improving organizational culture

Chapter 1: Assessing Your Current Culture

- Identifying the current culture in your organization
- Conducting a culture audit to evaluate strengths and weaknesses
- Gathering feedback from employees and stakeholders
- Analyzing data to identify areas for improvement

Chapter 2: Defining Your Desired Culture

- Creating a clear vision of the desired organizational culture
- Defining core values and behaviors that align with the vision
- Identifying the benefits of a positive culture for the organization and its stakeholders

Chapter 3: Leadership's Role in Shaping Culture

- The importance of leadership in creating and sustaining a positive culture
- Strategies for leaders to model the desired culture and behaviors

- Developing leaders' skills in promoting the desired culture

Chapter 4: Communication and Transparency

- The role of communication in building a positive culture
- Strategies for promoting open and transparent communication
- The importance of providing regular feedback to employees

Chapter 5: Employee Engagement and Recognition

- The importance of employee engagement in creating a positive culture
- Strategies for engaging employees in the vision and values of the organization
- The impact of recognition and rewards on employee motivation and satisfaction

Chapter 6: Diversity, Equity, and Inclusion

- The significance of DEI in building a positive and inclusive culture
- Strategies for promoting diversity and inclusion in the workplace
- The importance of equity in creating a fair and just workplace

Chapter 7: Sustaining a Positive Culture

- The challenges of sustaining a positive culture over time
- Strategies for monitoring and adjusting the culture as the organization evolves
- The role of continuous learning and improvement in building a positive culture

Conclusion:

- Recap of the key strategies for improving organizational culture
- The benefits of a positive culture for the organization and its stakeholders
- Call to action for leaders to prioritize culture building as a key organizational priority.

Preface

Once upon a time, in a bustling office, the employees were known for their fantastic camaraderie and positive culture. They were always quick to praise each other, provide support, and collaborate on tasks.

One day, the CEO of the company decided to introduce a new initiative to encourage positivity in the office - a "compliment box." The idea was simple: employees could write anonymous compliments about their colleagues and put them in the box, which would be opened and read aloud at the end of each week.

The first few weeks were a roaring success, with the box overflowing with heartfelt compliments and the team feeling more connected than ever. But then, something strange started to happen.

The compliments became increasingly absurd and nonsensical. "I admire your impressive ability to eat a sandwich," read one note. "Your hair reminds me of a majestic alpaca," said another. The team started to suspect that someone was playing a prank on them, but no one knew who it could be.

Finally, after weeks of this odd behavior, the CEO decided to investigate. He followed the trail of clues and eventually discovered that the culprit was none other than the office cat, who had learned how to open the box and had been stealing the compliment cards to use as toys.

Despite the odd turn of events, the team found themselves laughing and bonding over the silly antics of their feline friend. And in the end, they realized that maintaining a positive culture isn't just about formal initiatives and programs - sometimes, it's the unexpected moments of humor and connection that make all the difference.

Introduction

Organizational culture can be defined as the set of shared values, beliefs, attitudes, and behaviors that define how things are done within an organization. It encompasses everything from the way people communicate and make decisions to the way they dress and interact with one another.

Culture plays a critical role in shaping employee motivation, productivity, and retention. A positive and supportive culture can help employees feel valued, engaged, and invested in their work, leading to better performance and job satisfaction. On the other hand, a toxic or dysfunctional culture can erode morale, fuel conflicts, and drive talented employees away.

Improving organizational culture is not only a matter of creating a more pleasant workplace environment; it is a strategic imperative for any organization that wants to thrive in today's highly competitive and rapidly changing business landscape. By fostering a positive and inclusive culture, organizations can attract and retain top talent, foster innovation and creativity, build strong relationships with customers and other stakeholders, and achieve long-term success.

In this book, we will explore the key strategies and best practices for improving organizational culture. We will examine the role of leadership in shaping culture, the importance of communication and transparency, the power of employee engagement and recognition, and the significance of diversity, equity, and inclusion. Whether you are an executive, manager, or HR professional, this book will provide you with the knowledge and tools you need to create a culture that fosters success, well-being, and growth for your organization and its people.

Chapter 1:

Assessing Your Current Culture

"Assessing culture is like peeling an onion, you must peel off the layers to get to the core."

A culture audit is a critical first step in the process of improving organizational culture. Before you can make any meaningful changes, you need to understand the current culture of your organization. This chapter will explore the steps involved in conducting a culture audit, including identifying the current culture, gathering feedback from employees and stakeholders, and analyzing data to identify areas for improvement.

Identifying the Current Culture, the first step in assessing your current culture is to identify the underlying beliefs, values, and behaviors that define the way things are done in your organization. This may involve examining your organization's history, mission statement, and strategic plan, as well as talking to employees and observing their interactions.

There are several different ways to identify your current culture, including:

- Artifacts: These are the visible symbols of your organization's culture, such as the way people dress, the layout of the office, and the types of technology that are used. Artifacts can provide important clues about your organization's culture, but they may not always be an accurate reflection of what's really going on beneath the surface.

- Espoused Values: These are the beliefs and values that your organization claims to hold. They may be expressed in your mission statement, your strategic plan, or in other formal communications. However, espoused values may not always be consistent with the actual behaviors and practices that are observed in the organization.

- Enacted Values: These are the values and behaviors that are actually practiced by employees and managers in the organization. They may be seen in the way people make decisions, the way they interact with one another, or the way they prioritize their work.

By examining these different aspects of your organization, you can gain a better understanding of the current culture and identify areas where there may be gaps between the espoused values and the enacted values.

Conducting a Culture Audit

Once you have a clear understanding of the current culture in your organization, the next step is to conduct a culture audit to evaluate the strengths and weaknesses of your culture. A culture audit is a comprehensive process that involves gathering feedback from employees and stakeholders, as well as analyzing data to identify areas for improvement.

Airbnb, in 2016, following a series of controversies related to discrimination on its platform, the company undertook a comprehensive review of its culture and practices. The culture audit was led by former Attorney General Eric Holder and included interviews with hundreds of employees, as well as a review of company policies and practices.

The goal of the culture audit was to identify areas where the company's culture was falling short and to develop strategies for addressing those issues. The audit identified several key areas for improvement, including:

- Diversity and Inclusion: The audit found that the company's workforce lacked diversity, particularly at the senior levels, and that there were concerns about discrimination and bias on the platform. To address these issues, the company implemented a series of initiatives to increase diversity and promote inclusion, including unconscious bias training for employees and a commitment to hiring more women and underrepresented minorities.

- Accountability: The audit found that there was a lack of accountability within the organization, particularly around issues related to discrimination and harassment. To address this issue, the company implemented new reporting mechanisms for employees to report concerns, as well as a system for tracking and monitoring those reports.

- Communication: The audit found that there were issues with communication within the organization, particularly between employees and senior leadership. To address this issue, the company implemented regular town hall meetings and other communication channels to facilitate open dialogue between employees and leadership.

Following the culture audit, Airbnb implemented a series of changes to address the issues identified in the audit. These changes included new hiring and retention strategies to increase diversity, a commitment to transparency and accountability, and a renewed focus on communication and employee engagement. The company has since been recognized for its efforts to improve its culture and practices, including being named one of Fortune's "Best Workplaces for Diversity" in 2019.

The following are some of the key steps involved in conducting a culture audit:

- Define the scope and objectives: Before you begin, you need to define the scope and objectives of your culture audit. This may involve identifying the key areas that you want to assess, such as communication, leadership, or employee engagement. You may also want to set specific goals for the audit, such as identifying the top three areas for improvement.

- Gather feedback from employees: One of the most important sources of information for your culture audit is your employees. They are the ones who live and breathe your organization's culture every day, and they can provide valuable insights into what is working well and what needs to be improved. You can gather feedback through surveys, focus groups, interviews, or other methods.

- Engage stakeholders: In addition to employees, it's important to engage other stakeholders in your culture audit, such as customers, partners, and suppliers. They can provide a different perspective on your organization's culture and help you identify areas where you may be falling short.

- Analyze data: Once you have gathered feedback from employees and stakeholders, it's important to analyze the data to identify patterns and trends. This may involve using statistical analysis or other methods to identify the top areas for improvement.

- Create a culture audit report: Finally, you should create a culture audit report that summarizes the findings of your audit and provides recommendations for improvement. This report should be shared with key stakeholders in your organization, including executives, managers, and employees.

Analyzing Data to Identify Areas for Improvement The key to a successful culture audit is analyzing the data that you have collected to identify areas for improvement. There are several different methods you can use to analyze the data, including statistical analysis, qualitative analysis, and benchmarking.

Statistical analysis involves using quantitative methods to identify patterns and trends in your data. This may involve analyzing survey responses using tools like regression analysis or factor analysis. Statistical analysis can help you identify the factors that are most strongly associated with positive or negative cultural outcomes, such as employee engagement or turnover.

Qualitative analysis, on the other hand, involves analyzing the subjective data that you have collected, such as open-ended survey responses or comments from focus groups. This can be a more time-consuming process, but it can also provide rich insights into the nuances of your organization's culture.

Benchmarking involves comparing your organization's culture to that of other organizations in your industry or geographic region. This can help you identify areas where you may be falling behind your peers and provide guidance on best practices for improvement.

Once you have analyzed the data, you should be able to identify the top areas for improvement in your organization's culture. This may include improving communication and transparency, developing stronger leadership skills, fostering greater employee engagement, or promoting diversity, equity, and inclusion.

In conclusion, assessing your current culture is a critical first step in the process of improving organizational culture. By identifying the underlying beliefs, values, and behaviors that define your organization, and gathering feedback from employees and stakeholders, you can gain a clear understanding of the strengths and weaknesses of your culture. By analyzing the data that you have collected, you can identify areas for improvement and develop a plan to create a more positive, inclusive, and productive culture for your organization.

Chapter 2:

Defining Your Desired Culture

> "Culture is the invisible thread that weaves together the fabric of an organization, creating either a warm blanket or a scratchy wool sweater."

A positive organizational culture is essential for the success of any business. It contributes to employee motivation, productivity, and retention, which ultimately impact the bottom line. However, creating a positive culture is not easy. It requires a deliberate effort and a clear vision of what the desired culture looks like. In this chapter, we will discuss how to define your desired culture, including creating a clear vision, defining core values and behaviors, and identifying the benefits of a positive culture.

Creating a Clear Vision

Creating a clear vision of the desired organizational culture is the first step towards building a positive culture. It is essential to have a vision that is aspirational, inspirational, and achievable. The vision should be aligned with the organization's mission and values, and it should be communicated effectively to all employees.

In 2014, Microsoft underwent a major culture shift under the leadership of CEO Satya Nadella. Nadella recognized that the company's culture had become stagnant and needed to evolve to keep up with the changing tech industry.

Nadella's vision was to create a culture that was focused on innovation, collaboration, and a growth mindset. He believed that by empowering employees to take risks and learn from failures, the company could become more innovative and successful.

To bring this vision to life, Nadella implemented a series of initiatives to shift the company's culture. These initiatives included:

- Empowering employees: Nadella believed that to foster innovation, employees needed to feel empowered to take risks and try new things. He encouraged employees to experiment and learn from failures, rather than punishing them for mistakes.

- Collaboration: Nadella believed that collaboration was key to innovation, and he implemented initiatives to break down silos within the organization and encourage cross-functional teams to work together.

- Diversity and Inclusion: Nadella recognized that a diverse workforce was essential to innovation and success, and he implemented initiatives to increase diversity and promote inclusion within the company.

- Customer focus: Nadella believed that a focus on the customer was essential to driving innovation and success. He encouraged employees to listen to customer feedback and prioritize customer needs in their work.

By creating a clear vision for the company's culture and implementing initiatives to bring that vision to life, Microsoft was able to shift its culture and become more innovative and successful. The company has since been recognized for its efforts to improve its culture, including being named one of Fortune's "Best Companies to Work For" in 2020.

To create a clear vision, you need to ask yourself and your team questions such as:

- What kind of culture do we want to create?
- What values and behaviors do we want to promote?
- What do we want our employees to say about working here?
- How will our culture contribute to our organizational goals?
- What will our culture look like in practice?

Once you have answered these questions, you can begin to articulate a vision statement that reflects your desired culture. This statement should be concise, memorable, and meaningful. It should inspire and motivate employees to work towards achieving the desired culture.

Defining Core Values and Behaviors

Defining core values and behaviors is essential for creating a positive culture. Values are the principles that guide behavior, and they should reflect the organization's beliefs and philosophy. Behaviors are the actions that support the values, and they should be observable, measurable, and actionable.

To define core values and behaviors, you need to involve employees from across the organization. This will ensure that the values and behaviors reflect the organization's diversity and promote inclusion. You can use various methods to involve employees, such as focus groups, surveys, or town hall meetings.

Patagonia, the outdoor clothing and gear company, is known for its strong company culture and commitment to environmental sustainability. Here are some of their core values:

1. Build the best product: Patagonia values quality and craftsmanship in their products and strives to make the best possible products for their customers.

2. Cause no unnecessary harm: Patagonia is committed to reducing their environmental footprint and minimizing harm to the planet.

3. Use business to inspire and implement solutions to the environmental crisis: Patagonia believes that businesses have a responsibility to address environmental issues, and they are committed to using their platform to inspire change.

4. Not bound by convention: Patagonia values creativity and innovation and encourages employees to think outside the box.

5. Unwavering in their mission: Patagonia is committed to their mission of environmental sustainability and will not compromise on their values.

These core values reflect Patagonia's commitment to environmental sustainability and provide a framework for their employees to work towards a shared vision. By living these values every day, Patagonia has been able to create a strong culture and a loyal customer base.

When defining values and behaviors, it is essential to ensure that they are:

- Aligned with the organization's mission and vision
- Reflective of the organization's culture
- Actionable and observable
- Measurable and accountable

Once you have defined core values and behaviors, you can use them to guide decision-making, behavior, and performance management. You can also communicate them to employees and stakeholders and use them as a basis for training and development.

Identifying the Benefits of a Positive Culture

Creating a positive organizational culture has many benefits for the organization and its stakeholders. These benefits include:

- Increased employee engagement and motivation
- Improved productivity and performance
- Reduced turnover and absenteeism
- Enhanced customer satisfaction and loyalty
- Greater innovation and creativity
- Improved reputation and brand image

Zappos, an online retailer that is known for its exceptional customer service and employee-centric culture, is a great example of the benefits of a positive organizational culture. By prioritizing the happiness and well-being of their employees, Zappos has been able to create a culture of trust, collaboration, and innovation. Some of the benefits of Zappos' positive organizational culture include:

- Increased employee engagement: Zappos' employees are highly engaged and committed to their work, which has translated into high levels of productivity and job satisfaction.
- Improved customer service: Zappos' employees are known for their exceptional customer service, which has helped the company to build a loyal customer base.
- Greater innovation: Zappos' culture of collaboration and openness has encouraged employees to share ideas and experiment with new approaches, leading to greater innovation and creativity.
- Better retention: Zappos' positive culture has helped to create a supportive and fulfilling work environment, leading to better retention of top talent.
- Higher profits: Zappos' commitment to creating a positive organizational culture has paid off in the form of higher profits, as the company has been able to attract and retain loyal customers and top talent.

Overall, the benefits of a positive organizational culture are clear, and can have a significant impact on the success and sustainability of a company.

A positive culture also contributes to a sense of community and belonging among employees, which promotes a sense of purpose and fulfillment. It creates a work environment that is inclusive, respectful, and supportive, which promotes employee well-being and mental health.

By identifying the benefits of a positive culture, you can create a compelling case for change and generate buy-in from employees and stakeholders. You can also use the benefits to measure the impact of your culture change initiatives and demonstrate the return on investment.

In conclusion, defining your desired culture is a critical step in the process of improving organizational culture. By creating a clear vision, defining core values and behaviors, and identifying the benefits of a positive culture, you can provide a clear direction for your culture change initiatives. You can also create a compelling case for change and generate buy-in from employees and stakeholders. By focusing on creating a positive culture, you can create an environment that promotes employee well-being, productivity, and innovation, and contributes to the success of your organization.

Chapter 3:

Leadership's Role in Shaping Culture

"A leader's actions shape the culture, just as the sculptor's hands mold the clay."

Leadership plays a critical role in creating and sustaining a positive organizational culture. Leaders set the tone for the organization, and their actions and behaviors influence the behavior of employees. In this chapter, we will discuss the importance of leadership in shaping culture, strategies for leaders to model the desired culture and behaviors and developing leaders' skills in promoting the desired culture.

The Importance of Leadership in Shaping Culture

Starbucks is a well-known coffee chain that has always placed a high priority on its culture. In 2008, the company was facing significant financial challenges, and Howard Schultz returned as CEO to turn things around. One of the first things he did was to focus on the company's culture.

Schultz believed that the company's success depended on the quality of its people and the strength of its culture. He set out to create a culture of warmth and belonging, where employees felt valued, and customers felt welcome. To do this, he established a set of core values, which included:

- Creating a culture of warmth and belonging, where everyone is welcome
- Acting with courage, challenging the status quo, and finding new ways to grow the business

- Being present, connecting with transparency, dignity, and respect
- Delivering our very best in all we do, holding ourselves accountable for results

Schultz also implemented a number of programs and initiatives to support this culture, such as offering health benefits and stock options to all employees and creating a college tuition reimbursement program. He also introduced a program called "My Starbucks Idea," which allowed customers to submit suggestions for new products and services.

Under Schultz's leadership, Starbucks was able to turn its financial performance around and re-establish itself as a leader in the coffee industry. This success was due in large part to the company's strong culture, which was created and sustained by Schultz's leadership.

Leadership is essential for creating and sustaining a positive organizational culture. Leaders set the tone for the organization, and their actions and behaviors influence the behavior of employees. They have the power to shape the culture by modeling the desired behaviors, setting expectations, and holding employees accountable.

Leaders also have the responsibility of ensuring that the organization's values and behaviors are aligned with its mission and vision. They need to communicate the vision and values clearly and consistently and ensure that they are integrated into all aspects of the organization's operations.

Leadership also plays a critical role in creating a culture of trust and transparency. They need to be open and honest with employees, share information, and encourage feedback. They also need to create an environment that supports diversity and inclusion and promotes respect and collaboration.

Strategies for Leaders to Model the Desired Culture and Behaviors

Leaders can model the desired culture and behaviors by demonstrating the values and behaviors they want to see in their employees. They need to be consistent in their actions and words and hold themselves accountable for their behavior. Here are some strategies for leaders to model the desired culture and behaviors:

- Communicate the vision and values: Leaders need to communicate the vision and values of the organization clearly and consistently. They need to explain why they are important and how they relate to the organization's mission and goals.

- Lead by example: Leaders need to model the desired behaviors by demonstrating them in their own behavior. For example, if the organization values respect, leaders need to treat employees and stakeholders with respect.

- Encourage feedback: Leaders need to create an environment that supports feedback and encourages open and honest communication. They need to listen to feedback and take appropriate action to address any issues.

- Celebrate success: Leaders need to celebrate success and recognize employees who demonstrate the desired behaviors. This reinforces the values and behaviors and promotes a positive culture.

Developing Leaders' Skills in Promoting the Desired Culture

Developing leaders' skills in promoting the desired culture is essential for creating and sustaining a positive culture. Leaders need to be trained in the skills and behaviors that are aligned with the organization's values and vision. Here are some strategies for developing leaders' skills in promoting the desired culture:

- Provide training: Leaders need to be trained in the skills and behaviors that are aligned with the organization's values and vision. This includes communication, feedback, conflict resolution, and other skills that promote a positive culture.

- Foster mentorship: Leaders need to have mentors or coaches who can provide guidance and support in promoting the desired culture. This can be internal or external to the organization.

- Encourage continuous learning: Leaders need to be encouraged to continuously learn and develop their skills. This can be through training, attending conferences or workshops, or reading relevant books and articles.

- Measure and reward success: Leaders need to be held accountable for promoting the desired culture. This can be achieved by measuring their success in promoting the desired culture and rewarding them for their achievements.

In conclusion, leadership plays a critical role in creating and sustaining a positive organizational culture. Leaders need to model the desired culture and behaviors, communicate the vision and values, encourage feedback, and celebrate success. They also need to be trained in the skills and behaviors that promote a positive culture and be held accountable for their behavior. By focusing on leadership development and modeling the desired behaviors, organizations

Chapter 4:

Communication and Transparency

"Communication is the glue that binds a positive culture together - without it, the pieces will fall apart."

Effective communication is essential for building a positive organizational culture. It helps to build trust, encourages collaboration, and fosters a sense of belonging among employees. In this chapter, we will discuss the role of communication in building a positive culture, strategies for promoting open and transparent communication, and the importance of providing regular feedback to employees.

The Role of Communication in Building a Positive Culture

Zappos, an online shoe and clothing retailer, has become well-known for its culture of exceptional customer service and employee engagement. One of the keys to this culture is the company's emphasis on communication and transparency.

Zappos has a culture of open and honest communication, both within the company and with its customers. For example, the company's customer service representatives are encouraged to spend as much time as necessary on the phone with customers, to truly understand their needs and provide personalized service. Additionally, the company's website includes a live chat feature, which allows customers to communicate directly with customer service representatives in real-time.

Internally, Zappos places a high priority on employee engagement and feedback. The company has an open-door policy, which encourages employees to share their ideas, concerns, and feedback with their managers and executives. Zappos also has a program called "Zappos Insights," which offers training and consulting services to other companies on topics such as culture, leadership, and customer service.

Zappos has found that this culture of communication and transparency has had a number of benefits. It has helped to create a sense of trust and transparency with customers, which has led to increased loyalty and repeat business. It has also helped to create a sense of community and engagement among employees, which has led to increased productivity, job satisfaction, and retention.

Overall, Zappos demonstrates how communication is essential for building a positive culture. By creating a culture of open and honest communication, the company has been able to establish strong relationships with both its customers and its employees, which has helped to drive its success.

Communication is the foundation of any relationship, and it is particularly important in the workplace. Effective communication is essential for building a positive culture because it helps to build trust, encourages collaboration, and fosters a sense of belonging among employees.

Effective communication also plays a critical role in promoting transparency and accountability. When employees feel that their leaders are open and honest with them, they are more likely to trust and respect them. This, in turn, creates a more positive and productive workplace culture.

Strategies for Promoting Open and Transparent Communication

Promoting open and transparent communication requires a deliberate effort from leaders. Here are some strategies that can be used to promote open and transparent communication:

- Foster a culture of openness: Leaders need to create a culture that values openness and transparency. This can be achieved by encouraging feedback and open communication, sharing information and data, and promoting a culture of trust and respect.

- Encourage two-way communication: Leaders need to encourage two-way communication, where employees are encouraged to share their thoughts and ideas, and leaders are receptive to feedback. This can be achieved through regular check-ins, town hall meetings, or other communication channels.

- Use multiple communication channels: Leaders need to use a variety of communication channels to reach different groups of employees. This can include email, newsletters, social media, video conferences, and other communication channels.

- Communicate regularly and consistently: Leaders need to communicate regularly and consistently to ensure that employees are informed and engaged. This can include regular updates on the organization's performance, strategic goals, and upcoming events.

The Importance of Providing Regular Feedback to Employees

Adobe, for example, uses a performance management system called Check-in that emphasizes frequent feedback and coaching. Rather than a traditional annual performance review, employees and managers have regular Check-in meetings to discuss progress, provide feedback, and set goals. These meetings can occur as frequently as every week or every month, depending on the team's needs.

This approach to feedback helps employees feel more connected to their work and their manager, and it provides opportunities for course correction and continuous improvement. Additionally, by providing regular feedback, employees are more likely to feel valued and engaged in their work, which can contribute to a positive organizational culture.

Providing regular feedback to employees is essential for building a positive culture. Feedback helps employees to understand their strengths and weaknesses, set goals, and improve their performance. It also helps to build trust and a sense of belonging among employees.

Leaders need to provide regular feedback to employees on their performance, behavior, and contributions. This can be achieved through regular check-ins, performance reviews, or other communication channels. Feedback should be specific, constructive, and actionable, and should focus on both the positive and negative aspects of the employee's performance.

In addition to providing regular feedback, leaders also need to encourage feedback from employees. This can be achieved through surveys, focus groups, or other communication channels. Feedback should be used to identify areas for improvement and to inform decisions about organizational culture.

Effective communication and transparency are essential for building a positive organizational culture. Leaders need to foster a culture of openness, encourage two-way communication, use multiple communication channels, and communicate regularly and consistently. They also need to provide regular feedback to employees and encourage feedback from employees. By promoting open and transparent communication, leaders can create a more positive and productive workplace culture.

Chapter 5:

Employee Engagement and Recognition

"Engaging employees is like watering a plant - it requires consistent attention and nurturing, but the rewards are a thriving and beautiful culture."

Employee engagement is a critical element in creating a positive organizational culture. Engaged employees are more committed, productive, and loyal to the organization. In this chapter, we will discuss the importance of employee engagement in creating a positive culture, strategies for engaging employees in the vision and values of the organization, and the impact of recognition and rewards on employee motivation and satisfaction.

The Importance of Employee Engagement in Creating a Positive Culture

Employee engagement is the degree to which employees are emotionally and mentally invested in their work and the organization. Engaged employees are passionate about their work, committed to the organization's goals, and eager to contribute to its success. They are more likely to stay with the organization, work harder, and provide better customer service.

Engaged employees are also more likely to promote a positive culture. They are more likely to work collaboratively with others, share knowledge and ideas, and take ownership of their work. They also tend to be more positive, optimistic, and solution-focused, which can help to create a more positive and productive workplace culture.

Patagonia is known for its commitment to environmental and social responsibility, and this commitment is reflected in its company culture.

One way that Patagonia fosters employee engagement is through its "Let My People Go Surfing" policy. This policy allows employees to take time off during the workday to surf or engage in other outdoor activities. This policy is grounded in the belief that employees who are engaged in activities they love outside of work are more likely to be engaged and committed to their work.

Patagonia also encourages employee engagement through its onboarding process. New employees are encouraged to immerse themselves in the company's culture, values, and mission. They are given opportunities to participate in volunteer events and are encouraged to use their unique skills and passions to contribute to the company's mission.

By prioritizing employee engagement, Patagonia has created a culture of passionate and committed employees who are invested in the company's mission and values. This has helped the company attract and retain top talent, as well as create a positive impact on society and the environment.

Strategies for Engaging Employees in the Vision and Values of the Organization

Engaging employees in the vision and values of the organization requires a deliberate effort from leaders. Here are some strategies that can be used to engage employees in the vision and values of the organization:

- Communicate the vision and values: Leaders need to communicate the organization's vision and values regularly and consistently. This can be achieved through meetings, newsletters, or other communication channels.

- Involve employees in the decision-making process: Leaders need to involve employees in the decision-making process to ensure that they have a stake in the organization's success. This can be achieved through focus groups, brainstorming sessions, or other participatory processes.

- Provide opportunities for growth and development: Leaders need to provide employees with opportunities for growth and development to ensure that they feel valued and invested in the organization's success. This can be achieved through training programs, mentorship, or other developmental opportunities.

The Impact of Recognition and Rewards on Employee Motivation and Satisfaction

Airbnb has a strong culture of innovation and collaboration, and it uses a variety of rewards and recognition programs to reinforce and promote this culture.

One of Airbnb's most well-known rewards programs is its "Airbnb Employee Experience Credits" program. This program gives employees a set number of credits each year to use towards booking an Airbnb stay anywhere in the world. The program is designed to encourage employees to use the Airbnb platform, to experience the company's product, and to connect with people and cultures from around the world.

Another example of Airbnb's rewards program is its "Champion Awards." These awards recognize employees who have gone above and beyond in demonstrating the company's values of innovation, collaboration, and community. Winners of the Champion Awards receive a cash prize, a trophy, and public recognition from senior leaders and peers.

These rewards and recognition programs help reinforce Airbnb's culture of innovation, collaboration, and community. By incentivizing employees to use the company's product and experience the world, Airbnb reinforces its values of openness and cultural curiosity. By recognizing and rewarding employees who embody the company's values, Airbnb reinforces its culture of collaboration and teamwork. Overall, these rewards programs help Airbnb build a strong and positive culture that attracts and retains top talent, and that supports the company's mission and vision.

Recognition and rewards are powerful motivators that can help to create a positive organizational culture. When employees feel recognized and rewarded for their contributions, they are more likely to be motivated, engaged, and satisfied with their work. This, in turn, can help to create a more positive and productive workplace culture.

Recognition and rewards can take many forms, including verbal praise, bonuses, promotions, and other forms of recognition. The key is to ensure that the recognition and rewards are aligned with the organization's vision and values and are consistent with the employee's contributions.

Employee engagement and recognition are essential for creating a positive organizational culture. Engaged employees are more committed, productive, and loyal to the organization, and they promote a more positive and productive workplace culture. Leaders need to engage employees in the vision and values of the organization and provide opportunities for growth and development. They also need to recognize and reward employees for their contributions to ensure that they feel valued and invested in the organization's success. By promoting employee engagement and recognition, leaders can create a more positive and productive workplace culture.

Chapter 6:

Diversity, Equity, and Inclusion

> "Diversity, equity, and inclusion are not just buzzwords; they are the building blocks of a culture that values every voice and empowers all to thrive."

Diversity, equity, and inclusion (DEI) are critical elements in building a positive and inclusive organizational culture. In this chapter, we will discuss the significance of DEI in building a positive and inclusive culture, strategies for promoting diversity and inclusion in the workplace, and the importance of equity in creating a fair and just workplace.

The Significance of DEI in Building a Positive and Inclusive Culture

DEI refers to the policies, practices, and culture that encourage and support diversity, equity, and inclusion in the workplace. A positive and inclusive culture promotes a sense of belonging and fosters a work environment where employees feel valued, respected, and supported.

A positive and inclusive culture is also critical for attracting and retaining a diverse workforce. It can help to foster creativity, innovation, and better decision-making. In a diverse workplace, employees can bring different perspectives, experiences, and backgrounds to the table, leading to more robust and inclusive solutions.

Salesforce, a leading customer relationship management (CRM) software company. Salesforce has a comprehensive approach to DEI and has implemented a variety of initiatives to create a more diverse, equitable, and inclusive workplace.

One key initiative is the company's "Ohana Groups," which are employee-led resource groups that focus on specific communities and interests, such as Black employees, LGBTQ+ employees, and employees with disabilities. These groups provide a safe and supportive space for employees to connect, share experiences, and advocate for change within the company.

Salesforce also has a robust training program focused on unconscious bias, diversity, and inclusion. All employees are required to complete this training, and the company offers additional resources for managers to help them create more inclusive teams.

In addition to these initiatives, Salesforce has committed to regularly reporting on its progress toward DEI goals and has set ambitious targets for increasing representation of underrepresented groups in the company.

These efforts have had a significant impact on Salesforce's culture. The company has been recognized as a top employer for diversity and inclusion, and employees report feeling more engaged and valued as a result of the company's DEI initiatives. By prioritizing DEI and creating a more inclusive workplace, Salesforce has built a culture that values and respects all employees, leading to improved morale and higher levels of employee retention.

Strategies for Promoting Diversity and Inclusion in the Workplace

Promoting diversity and inclusion in the workplace requires a concerted effort from leaders. Here are some strategies that can be used to promote diversity and inclusion in the workplace:

- Review and update policies and practices: Leaders need to review and update their policies and practices to ensure that they promote diversity and inclusion. This can include recruitment practices, promotion policies, and employee development programs.

- Provide training and education: Leaders need to provide training and education to employees to raise awareness about diversity and inclusion. This can include workshops, seminars, and online learning modules.

- Foster a sense of community: Leaders need to foster a sense of community in the workplace to promote inclusion. This can include social events, volunteer opportunities, and employee resource groups.

The Importance of Equity in Creating a Fair and Just Workplace

Equity refers to the fair and just distribution of resources and opportunities. In the workplace, equity means that all employees have an equal opportunity to succeed and that their contributions are valued and recognized. When employees feel that they are treated fairly and justly, they are more likely to be engaged, motivated, and committed to the organization's success.

In 2015, Intel announced a commitment to improving diversity and inclusion within the company and the tech industry.

To achieve this goal, Intel implemented several initiatives, such as:

1. Investing $300 million to increase the representation of women and underrepresented minorities in its workforce.

2. Creating an inclusive hiring program to attract diverse talent, including hosting hackathons and partnering with organizations focused on diversity in tech.

3. Providing unconscious bias training to all employees to help eliminate bias in the hiring process and daily interactions.

4. Creating a Diversity in Technology Initiative to encourage innovation and collaboration across diverse teams.

As a result of these initiatives, Intel saw significant improvements in its diversity and inclusion metrics. For example, the percentage of women in technical roles increased from 15.4% in 2014 to 26.8% in 2020, and the percentage of underrepresented minorities in technical roles increased from 9.8% in 2014 to 16.1% in 2020. Additionally, Intel has received recognition for its DEI efforts, such as being named one of DiversityInc's Top 50 Companies for Diversity in 2020. Overall, these efforts have helped to create a fairer and more just workplace for all employees at Intel.

Leaders need to ensure that their policies and practices promote equity in the workplace. This can include pay equity, access to training and development, and equal opportunities for promotion.

Diversity, equity, and inclusion are critical elements in building a positive and inclusive organizational culture. Leaders need to promote diversity and inclusion in the workplace through policies, practices, and culture. They also need to ensure that their workplace promotes equity and fairness to ensure that all employees have an equal opportunity to succeed. By promoting DEI, leaders can create a positive and inclusive workplace culture that fosters a sense of belonging, creativity, and innovation.

Chapter 7:

Sustaining a Positive Culture

"Sustaining a positive culture requires continuous effort and attention, like tending to a garden that must be watered and weeded regularly to thrive."

Building a positive organizational culture is not a one-time effort but a continuous process. In this chapter, we will discuss the challenges of sustaining a positive culture over time, strategies for monitoring and adjusting the culture as the organization evolves, and the role of continuous learning and improvement in building a positive culture.

The Challenges of Sustaining a Positive Culture over Time

Building a positive organizational culture is a continuous effort that requires ongoing commitment and dedication. The challenges of sustaining a positive culture over time can include complacency, resistance to change, and turnover of key personnel. As the organization evolves, its culture can also evolve, and leaders need to be aware of these changes to ensure that the culture remains aligned with the organization's values and goals.

the challenges to sustaining a positive culture is the rapid growth of an organization. As companies expand, their culture may become diluted, and it becomes more challenging to maintain consistency across different departments, teams, and locations.

For instance, when Google grew from a small start-up to a global technology giant, it faced challenges in maintaining its unique culture. As the company expanded, it became more challenging to maintain consistency in its culture, leading to issues such as high turnover rates and low employee satisfaction. To address these issues, Google implemented various strategies to ensure that its culture remained consistent and aligned with its values.

One of the strategies that Google used was to hire employees who shared its values and beliefs, ensuring that the culture remained intact as the company grew. The company also invested in training programs to help new employees understand and embrace the culture. Furthermore, Google regularly monitored and assessed its culture through surveys and feedback sessions, allowing it to identify any potential issues and take corrective action promptly.

Another challenge to sustaining a positive culture is the departure of key leaders or employees. When individuals who are instrumental in shaping the culture leave the company, it can be challenging to maintain the same level of culture and values. In such cases, it is essential to ensure that the values and culture are ingrained in the organization's DNA, so they are not solely dependent on individuals.

For example, when Starbucks' former CEO, Howard Schultz, stepped down from his position, there were concerns about how the company would maintain its positive culture. However, Starbucks had ingrained its culture and values throughout the organization, making it easier for new leaders to step in and continue to promote a positive culture. The company also invests heavily in training and development programs, ensuring that all employees understand and embody its culture.

Sustaining a positive culture can be challenging, particularly as organizations grow and evolve. However, it is possible to maintain consistency by hiring employees who share the organization's values, investing in training programs, regularly monitoring, and assessing the culture, and ensuring that the values and culture are ingrained in the organization's DNA.

Strategies for Monitoring and Adjusting the Culture as the Organization Evolves

To sustain a positive organizational culture, leaders need to monitor the culture and adjust it as the organization evolves. Here are some strategies that can be used to monitor and adjust the culture:

- Conduct regular culture assessments: Leaders can conduct regular culture assessments to evaluate the organization's culture and identify areas for improvement.

- Solicit feedback from employees and stakeholders: Leaders can solicit feedback from employees and stakeholders to gain insight into how the culture is perceived and identify areas for improvement.

- Adjust policies and practices: Leaders can adjust policies and practices to align with the desired culture and values.

The Role of Continuous Learning and Improvement in Building a Positive Culture

Continuous learning and improvement are critical in building and sustaining a positive organizational culture. Leaders need to be open to feedback and willing to learn from their mistakes. They also need to encourage their employees to learn and grow, providing opportunities for training and development.

Continuous learning and improvement can help leaders to stay up-to-date with best practices and new trends in culture management. It can also help employees to develop new skills and perspectives, which can contribute to a more innovative and inclusive workplace.

Building and sustaining a positive organizational culture is a continuous effort that requires ongoing commitment and dedication. Leaders need to monitor and adjust the culture as the organization evolves, using strategies such as regular culture assessments, soliciting feedback, and adjusting policies and practices. They also need to embrace continuous learning and improvement to stay up-to-date with best practices and new trends in culture management. By doing so, leaders can create a positive and inclusive workplace culture that fosters employee engagement, productivity, and success.

It is important to offer opportunities for employees to grow and flourish within an organization. One example of this is the Microsoft Aspire Experience program, which is designed to help early-career employees develop the skills and knowledge they need to succeed at the company. The program includes a range of training sessions, mentoring, coaching, and networking opportunities, all aimed at helping employees build their skills and gain new experiences.

In addition to formal training programs, Microsoft also encourages employees to pursue their own learning and development goals through initiatives such as online learning resources, access to industry events and conferences, and support for continuing education programs. By prioritizing continuous learning and development, Microsoft is able to create a culture that values growth, innovation, and long-term success.

Let's Recap

Organizational culture is a critical aspect of any organization and improving it can lead to significant benefits for the organization and its stakeholders. In this book, we have discussed various strategies for improving organizational culture, including assessing the current culture, defining the desired culture, leadership's role in shaping culture, communication and transparency, employee engagement and recognition, and diversity, equity, and inclusion. We have also discussed the challenges of sustaining a positive culture over time and the role of continuous learning and improvement in building a positive culture.

The benefits of a positive culture for the organization and its stakeholders are numerous. It can lead to increased employee engagement, productivity, and satisfaction, as well as improved customer satisfaction and loyalty. A positive culture can also contribute to a more innovative and inclusive workplace, attracting top talent and improving the organization's reputation.

As leaders, it is our responsibility to prioritize culture building as a key organizational priority. By investing in improving the organizational culture, we can create a workplace that supports the success and wellbeing of our employees while achieving our business goals. We must lead by example, model the desired behaviors, and empower our employees to embrace the values and vision of the organization.

Building and sustaining a positive organizational culture is a continuous process that requires ongoing commitment and dedication. However, by following the strategies outlined in this book, we can create a workplace culture that fosters employee engagement, productivity, and success, and leads to long-term benefits for the organization and its stakeholders.

By prioritizing the development of a positive culture, organizations can establish a strong foundation for growth and long-term success. As we have discussed in this book, creating a positive culture requires a comprehensive approach that involves leadership, communication, engagement, and continuous learning and improvement.

To achieve a positive culture, leaders must recognize the importance of their role in shaping the culture and model the desired behaviors for their employees. They must also provide opportunities for employees to provide feedback and ensure that communication is open and transparent. Recognition and rewards can also play a vital role in promoting employee engagement and satisfaction.

Finally, creating a culture of diversity, equity, and inclusion is essential to creating a positive culture. By valuing and promoting diversity in the workplace, organizations can build a culture that is more innovative and inclusive, leading to better outcomes for the organization and its employees.

In conclusion, building a positive culture is a critical aspect of organizational success. Leaders must prioritize culture building as a key organizational priority and invest in the strategies that we have discussed in this book to achieve a positive and sustainable culture. By doing so, organizations can attract and retain top talent, foster innovation, and achieve long-term success.

Appendix

Culture Assessment Survey

We appreciate your honest feedback on our organization's culture. Your answers will help us understand the strengths and areas of improvement for our culture. Please answer the following questions honestly and anonymously.

1. How satisfied are you with our organization's culture?

- Very satisfied
- Satisfied
- Neutral
- Dissatisfied
- Very dissatisfied

2. How would you describe our organization's culture in one word?

3. What are the values you believe our organization should embody?

4. Do you feel like you belong in our organization?

- Strongly agree
- Agree
- Neutral
- Disagree
- Strongly disagree

5. How often do you receive recognition and feedback for your work?
- Daily
- Weekly
- Monthly
- Rarely
- Never

6. How well does our organization encourage and support diversity, equity, and inclusion?
- Very well
- Well
- Neutral
- Poorly
- Very poorly

7. Do you feel that our organization provides ample opportunities for growth and development?
- Strongly agree
- Agree
- Neutral
- Disagree
- Strongly disagree

8. How well do our leaders model and promote the desired culture and behaviors?

- Very well
- Well
- Neutral
- Poorly
- Very poorly

9. Do you feel comfortable providing feedback or raising concerns to your supervisor or manager?

- Yes, always
- Yes, sometimes
- No, rarely
- No, never

10. What is one thing that our organization can do to improve the culture?

Thank you for taking the time to complete this survey. Your feedback is valuable to us, and we appreciate your commitment to making our organization a better place to work.

Leaders' Pledge for Building a Positive Culture

As a leader in this organization, I commit to building and sustaining a positive culture that promotes the well-being and success of all employees. I understand that culture is not just an abstract concept, but a tangible force that shapes our actions and outcomes every day. Therefore, I pledge to:

1. Model the behaviors and values that align with our desired culture and hold myself and others accountable for upholding them.

2. Communicate openly and transparently with employees, sharing information and feedback that promotes trust, respect, and collaboration.

3. Foster an inclusive and diverse workplace, where everyone feels valued and respected, and has equal opportunities to grow and succeed.

4. Recognize and reward employees' contributions and achievements and celebrate the milestones and successes of our organization.

5. Continuously learn and improve my own skills and knowledge related to culture building, and support employees' learning and growth as well.

By making this pledge, I am committed to creating a workplace that inspires and energizes employees, fosters innovation and excellence, and contributes positively to our communities and society. I am proud to be a leader in this organization and look forward to working with all of you to build a better culture for us all.

Congratulations on reaching the end of this book! Remember, building a positive culture is an ongoing process that requires dedication, effort, and continuous learning. Stay committed to your vision, listen to your employees, and don't be afraid to make adjustments along the way. Cultivating a positive culture is not only good for your organization, but it also has a positive impact on your employees, customers, and community. Good luck on your journey, and may your culture thrive!

www.ingramcontent.com/pod-product-compliance
Lightning Source LLC
Chambersburg PA
CBHW070801220526
45467CB00017B/700